Meditation Series : 1

MW00469961

Morning Meditation Prayers

"One has to see the beauty of prayer.
There is no meditation, no ritual, without prayer.
There is no technique that can replace prayer
Because in any technique the will is retained.
Here, the will willingly submits.
The submission performs the miracle."

Swami Dayananda Saraswati
Arsha Vidya

Arsha Vidya
Research and Publication Trust
Chennai

Published by :
Arsha Vidya Research
and Publication Trust
32 / 4 ' Sri Nidhi ' Apts III Floor
Sir Desika Road Mylapore
Chennai 600 004 INDIA
Tel   : 044 2499 7023
Telefax: 2499 7131
Email : avrandpc@gmail.com

ISBN : 978 – 93 – 80049 – 04 – 5

Revised Edition : May 2009 Copies : 3000

Design :
Suchi Ebrahim

Printed by :
Sudarsan Graphics
27, Neelakanta Mehta Street
T. Nagar, Chennai 600 017
Email : info@sudarsan.com

Preface

Human free will finds total expression in a quiet voluntary prayer. At these prayerful moments what I feel and say are very important. The fact that I can pray is itself a blessing, and how I pray makes prayer meaningful to me.

The past seems to have a tight hold on each of us. To let go our past is merely wishful thinking. It does not happen. If we can have a degree of awareness of this problem, we can discover hope and solution in a well-directed prayer.

These few pages bring to you some of the meditation prayers I conducted for the students of the *gurukula*. When you read them, be with the words and keep seeing their meaning.

Swami Dayananda Saraswati
April 27 2009
Coimbatore

The following series of guided morning meditation prayers, based on the Serenity prayers of Alchoholics Anonymous, was conducted by Swami Dayananda Saraswati for the students attending a three-year resident course in Vedanta and Sanskrit at Arsha Vidya Gurukulam, Saylorsburg, Pennsylvania, U.S.A.

As a limited individual, I invoke the Lord's help, the Lord's grace, by an act of prayer. Being based on one's will, prayer is an action. It is an act invoking grace as well as simple auto-suggestion. As I sit in meditation, relaxed, I offer a prayer to the Lord whom I invoke in any given form, in any given name. I pray.

> O Lord
> May I have the maturity to accept gracefully what I cannot change; may I have the will and effort to change what I can; and may I have the wisdom to know the difference between what I can and cannot change.

I cannot change my childhood, my parentage and my entire past. What has happened in my life, I cannot change. What has happened has happened. I cannot do anything about it. On the basis of what has happened, I have nothing to regret. I have no reason to be sad, depressed or angry. I drop my anguish for what has happened. I accept gracefully whatever has happened in my life.

There are lot of things that I can change and repair. I seek the strength of will and the ability to make proper, adequate efforts to change. I do not waste my time trying to change what I cannot change; nor do I waste my time putting up with unhealthy situations that I can change. The difference between the two, what I can and cannot change, is not easy to distinguish. It takes wisdom for which I again invoke your grace.

> *O Lord*
> *May I enjoy, have*
> *The maturity to accept*
> *Gracefully what I cannot change*
> *The will and effort to change*
> *What I can*
> *And the wisdom to know the difference.*

I am awake, alive to what happens at this moment. I lay down my will, my choice. I am awake to the moment. Moment to moment, my being aware of the moment does not fluctuate. My being aware of the moment is an abiding, lasting, ever-present fact. My being aware is not in fits and starts. It is a presence, a presence which is always present.

What I am aware of at this moment is unique. The object changes; even these words are never the same. At this moment, a given word, a sentence, a sound or an object, changes. My being aware of what happens at this moment is not by choice. I am aware because I am an awareful presence. Free from memory, I am an awareful presence.

2

As an individual with a limited mind, a set of senses and a body, I play different roles every day. As son, husband, father, uncle, friend, employer and so on, I play different roles. All these roles are played by me, the individual.

When I think of my father, I am a son. When I think of my friend, I am a friend. In order to be a friend, I replace my father with my friend.

My relationship with the Lord is not the same. As an individual I am fundamentally related to the Lord, whether I recognise the relationship or not. This relationship is expressed by the word 'devotee'.

As a devotee, when I assume the role of father or son, the devotee is not replaced. The relationship between me, the individual, and the Lord, is the same as that between my father and the Lord or my friend and the Lord. The devotee remains due to the abiding nature of the relationship with the Lord. The relationship is an abiding relationship, a fundamental relationship born of recognition. As a person, an individual, I see myself a devotee. A relationship that exists with the Lord is recognised. Only then does religion have meaning.

As a devotee, I express my devotion in various forms. As a devotee, I invoke the help and the grace of the Lord by an act of prayer. Prayer is an action. Its result is what is called grace. I create the grace through the act of prayer. I require grace to remove obstacles, problems and difficulties. My efforts themselves are supported by the grace I win or earn. I invoke the grace of the Lord or I invoke the Lord.

> *O Lord*
> *May I have the capacity, the maturity*
> *To accept gracefully*
> *What I cannot change*
> *The will and effort to change*
> *What I can*
> *And the wisdom to know the difference.*

As a child, I was helpless. My will was not with me. My mind was not informed enough to see, to interpret. Whatever happened to me as a child and later in life, I cannot do anything about. It happened in the past; it is past.

What has happened has happened. Maybe there is a meaning to it all. Maybe the meaning is that I can now pray. Maybe all that happened has made me what I am today.

May I accept gracefully what has happened in the past. May I have the maturity to do so. There are lot of things I can change. I can change my attitudes toward the world and myself. I can tighten up my personal life if it is loose. If it is too tight, I can loosen up. I can repair any damage done. May I enjoy the will, not merely an intention or a desire, but a will supported by adequate effort. May I have the will and effort to change what I can, wherever I have to. And may I have the wisdom to know what I can and cannot change.

May I not victimise myself by subjecting myself to the past. Let me see clearly that I cannot alter what has happened. May I not have any regret, sadness, anger, or agitation on this score. Let me recognise very clearly all my thoughts about the past that I cannot change, so that I can accept the past for what it is. Let me be aware of whatever I can change. Let it be clear to me. Let there be no doubt. Let me not waste my power and time trying to change what I cannot change. Trying to change what I cannot change leaves me so powerless, helpless and impoverished, that I cannot bring about the required change.

O Lord, may I have the maturity to accept totally, gracefully, what I cannot change, the will and effort to change what I can, and the knowledge

of the difference between what I can and cannot
change.

That you are not the past
You see by being awareful
Of the present

The present moment
You are aware of
You are an awareful presence

In the awareful presence that you are
Perceptions happen
The objects of perception
Are many and various

You are an awareful presence
An abiding awareful presence.

3

I do not want to be a victim of my own past. If I hold on to the past, I can drop it. I can let it go. Like an object in my hand, I can just drop it. However, the problem is that the past holds me. I am helpless. When the past holds me, the past and I are so united, so identical, that the past itself becomes I. It seems to hold me hostage.

In my ignorance and innocence, I subjected myself to hurt, guilt, and therefore pain. I remain associated with these memories. Some of these memories may not be vivid, but they form the very I. I find myself helpless in letting go of the past.

If someone holds me, I can seek someone's help to free myself. But here, the one who holds, the held, and the holding itself are identical. I have to either plead to myself or to the Lord. In pleading, imploring, there is submission. There is an acknowledgment on my part that I am helpless. The submission of my helplessness to the Lord is real prayer.

Such a prayer, implying acknowledgment of helplessness and submission to the Lord, brings about the conversion of letting the past go. In the submission is the acknowledgment. The completeness of the acknowledgment takes place in the submission and the submission takes place when I pray, consciously pray. Prayer is not a technique. It is an action, no doubt, but it is not a technique. It is born of an acknowledgment of my helplessness.

> *O Lord*
> *Help me to let go the past*
> *Let me not try to change*
> *What I cannot*
>
> *When I blame someone*
> *I do not let go*
> *I want to change*
> *What I cannot change*

In blaming, there is no acceptance of a fact. There is an attempt to change what I cannot.

> *O Lord*
> *Let me not blame anyone*
> *What has happened*
> *Is a fact*
> *It remains a fact*
> *I cannot do anything about it*
> *I do not have remorse*
> *Resentment or anger*

O Lord
Let me not try
To change
What I cannot change

May I have the will
To back up my desire
To fulfil my will

May I have adequate effort
To change what I can
May I have no confusion
With reference to what I can
And cannot change
I implore your help.

4

I bring Īśvara, the Lord, into my life when I recognise my helplessness, uncertainty, and incapacity to order things as I want. There is uncertainty with reference to the fulfilment of my wishes and desires. There are limitations of strength in terms of will and the capacity to make the necessary effort. There are also limitations in terms of knowledge and resources. There is absence of freedom in my mental life. Recognition of this makes me acknowledge my helplessness.

Recognition itself reveals a degree of maturity. I seek further maturity by invoking the grace, the invisible and the intangible, something that makes things possible. I invoke the grace of the Lord to accept things that I cannot change. My sorrows, agitations and anger, leading to depression, stem from my not accepting and understanding the past.

> O Lord, I have blamed a number of factors, people, situations, time, places and society. Perhaps all of these have helped me to come to the point where I can pray. I realise that no one is to blame nor do I blame myself. May I

gracefully and totally accept what I cannot change. I can change my attitudes and work for the necessary understanding. I can bring a better order to my personal life. I can make whatever effort is necessary. O Lord, may I have the will and effort to change what I can. May I know what I can and cannot change.

More often I lay waste my powers and my time to change what I cannot change. And when I have to change what I can, I am already tired. I am impoverished in terms of will, energy, effort and the capacity for effort. May I have the knowledge to know the difference between the two: what I can and cannot change.

One by one find out what you want to change; list them.

I wish my father had a different attitude. I wish my mother had a different mental make-up and more personal discipline. I wish I had studied more. I wish my home was a real home. I wish I had understood the value of values. I wish I had been more disciplined. I wish I had heeded the words of advice of so and so. I wish I had not met this person. I wish I had not done a particular action. I wish I had done a particular action. I wish I had equipped myself with some skills and better titles. I wish I had been born under another astrological sign. I wish I had been born a male. I wish I had been born a female. I wish I had not been born at all.

How many resentments
And useless wishes!

O Lord
Help me understand
Intimately
The uselessness
Of these wishes
Help me drop
Every one of them.

5

As an individual I see myself a victim of my past. I honestly acknowledge the fact that the past holds me and determines my mental condition. I see myself as a hostage of the past. I acknowledge the fact and I also acknowledge my helplessness. If I can help myself I will not be a victim of my past. Depression, fear, anger, self-criticism, intolerance, hatred, unhappiness, if I am not a victim I will not have any of them. These conditions reveal my helplessness. They do not happen without the past. If I can help myself I will not have them.

Once I see and honestly acknowledge my helplessness, I can seek help. I seek help not at the altars of the world. I have sought there before. I now seek help from a source I look upon as a being of all knowledge, of all power, whom I call the Lord, Īśvara. I establish a contact, a relationship with Īśvara through prayer. As a child I went to my mother or father for help. Now, as an adult, I go to the source of everything. Freely, I go to the source. I am not shy. I acknowledge my helplessness. I seek help through prayer.

I pray for strength, clarity, serenity to accept gladly, gracefully, what I cannot change. When I blame a situation or person for my being what I am, mother, father, friend, boss, death, poverty, society, political/economic systems, my stars, health, institutions, schools, colleges, media or music, when I blame any one of them, I must know that I do not accept my past. In blaming there is resentment of a fact. There is rejection of a fact. But a fact is a fact. My rejection does not alter it. It only adds to my confusion.

In order to accept gracefully what I cannot change, I blame no one. I blame neither the situation nor myself. I am not to blame. I let go of the past. I totally accept all situations and people who have come into my past, who have perhaps contributed to my past, who have caused my past. At this stage, I may not appreciate why these people did what they did. I may not appreciate their problems to be what they were, what they are, but at least I do not blame them because I accept my past.

Whatever has happened is a fact. I cannot but accept it. My rejection does not change the fact or negate it. I accept gracefully and blame no one. All I seek is maturity, clarity, a space within me from where I gracefully accept what I cannot change.

I also seek help for adequate will in order to bring about changes, desirable changes, in my attitude towards people, money, the future, my health, my body, my skills, and healthy proper attitudes.

If I have to bring about any other change or if I have to apply myself in order to learn more, I pray.

O Lord
Please give me
The unflinching will
The will that holds
Against all odds
An unflinching will
To change

May I also have the knowledge
To know what I can
And cannot change
Knowledge that helps me
Accept what I cannot change

Once I know
Something cannot be changed
I can accept it

And once I know
I can change
I can do what needs to be done
May I have this knowledge.

6

The basis for any form of prayer is not one's helplessness; it is the acknowledgment of one's helplessness. The key to an efficacious prayer is realizing my helplessness. Prayer is born naturally when I realise my helplessness and also recognise the source of all Power, all knowledge. if both of these are acknowledged, prayer is very natural.

If everything is in order I need not pray. All prayers have their fulfilment in keeping everything in order. If everything is in order, prayer becomes redundant. My prayers have already been answered.

When I am helpless, I seek help from any person I can. When the helplessness is in terms of my incapacity to let go of my past or to let us the future happen without my being apprehensive, then no outside help from a person like myself is of any use. I go to the source from where such help is possible. I invoke the Lord in prayer.

I intimately realise that I am a victim of my own past. As a victim of my past, I cannot but be apprehensive about the future. I become worried. I become cautious. I become frightened of my future. To deliver myself into the hands of the Lord, I deliver myself to the order that is the Lord. The Lord is not separate from the order and the order is not separate from the Lord. My past then becomes part of the meaningful order of my personal life. The future unfolds itself in keeping with the same order, an order that includes my previous karma, if there is such a thing.

All's well that shapes well, that ends well. Past mistakes become meaningful as long as they have made me wiser. To acknowledge my helplessness is in itself a great step towards recognising the order. I intimately acknowledge my immediate past and remove the past from my life.

As a child I had no will of my own. I was in the hands of my parents, my elders, my teachers and other adult members of the society. As a child, I see that I was absolutely helpless. My knowledge was limited and my perception was never clear. I was insecure. I was learning with a small mind and with meagre information, without any worldly wisdom, without any wisdom at all. Naturally, I made conclusions about the world and myself. Those conclusions formed the basis for my interpretation of the events to come. In the process, these interpreted events definitely seem to confirm my conclusions.

Look at the helplessness. As an adult I cannot remove the conclusions I made as a child and therefore I become a victim of my own past. Whom should I blame? I cannot blame myself. Nor can I afford to blame the world. Blaming is to retain the past and does not help me let go. It is one thing to acknowledge the mistakes of others but quite another to hold on to them and retain my fears and anger. I have to eliminate all forms of blame in order to be free of my past.

I may have valid reasons to blame. I see those reasons and I let go of my past. By allowing my blaming to continue, I allow the past to continue. If I was a victim of the behaviour of my elders, by blaming them now I continue to be a victim. I Understand it all, but still I am helpless.

> *O Lord*
> *Help me accept gracefully*
> *What I cannot change*
> *Let me be free of blaming anyone*
> *Including myself*
> *I cannot blame myself*
> *For what happened to me*
>
> *Nor can I blame others because*
> *Others themselves have others to blame*
> *Help me accept gracefully*
> *What I cannot change*
>
> *Blaming means*
> *I want to change the past*

I want my past to be different
How can it be?

O Lord
Help me accept gracefully
What I cannot change
I let go of my resentment
Anger and dissatisfaction
By accepting gracefully
What I cannot change

O Lord
Perhaps what I went through
Was meant to happen
Perhaps it was all in order
For it has given me
The ability to pray

The years of pain
Struggle
Groping
Seem to have paid off
For I am able to pray

And by prayer
Everything
has become meaningful

My pain
My past
Has resulted
In my coming to you
To seek help

Intimately
I acknowledge
My helplessness

I seek your help
Your intervention
To make me drop
What I cannot change
To make me accept
What I cannot change
Which even you cannot change

You cannot change
What has happened
Nor can I
Nor anyone else
Intimately I acknowledge
The fact that what has happened
Cannot be changed

O Lord
Help me totally
Accept what I cannot change
My mother's behaviour
Her omissions and commissions
My father's neglect
His anger and indifference
His lack of care
His mishandling and mismanagement
His drinking
The fights between them
The confusion at home
My being left alone
Not fondled
Not cared for

This is how I felt
Not cared for
Not loved
I was wrong perhaps
But it was how I felt

O Lord
I cannot change
What has happened

Please help me accept gracefully
What I cannot change
I do not want to bury the past
Nor do I want to forget the past
I cannot

I just want to accept the fact
Accept the past

Gracefully
I accept the past
I even begin to see
An order in all of this
For do I not pray now?

I have come to be objective
I see some order here

O Lord
Please help me accept gracefully
What I cannot change.

7

Problems such as anger, depression, sadness, self-criticism and self-dissatisfaction, for the most part stem from one's childhood. I am not to blame for these problems. The outside world is to blame, parents, teachers, other elders and society consisting of a number of people, situations and events. All these are to blame. Either we blame ourselves illegitimately or blame others legitimately.

I free myself from blaming myself. I am not to blame for what happened to me as a child. As a child I was helpless. I did not have the necessary knowledge or information with which to understand, to take action appropriate to each situation. When someone else was to blame, I did not have the knowledge to say, 'You are wrong.' I thought I was wrong. I was not an adult, therefore could not make decisions and act upon them. Others had to make decisions and do things that affected me. I am not to blame.

I free myself from blaming others also. If I blame others, then I still carry the past. As long as I continue to blame, the factors that cause damage to me continue. The 'I' that was subject to pain continues to be, along with the anger and resentment.

I cannot forget my past. How can I? I know what has happened. How can I forget? To bury the past is easier said than done. No one can bury one's past. All I can do is to accept the past gracefully. I cannot afford to blame any one or anything. Nor can I afford to blame myself. Even as an adult, any omission or commission on my part was determined by the helpless 'I' that was the child. I see that I am not to blame. I also see the uselessness of blaming others.

I gracefully accept the past because I cannot afford to blame. Perhaps there was a meaning to all that has happened in my life. All is well that ends well. Whatever happened to me might be in order because now I am ready to accept the entire past gracefully. People do not accept what has happened, even in their old age. My pleading to the Lord, 'Please help me accept this situation,' makes the entire past meaningful.

> Please help me, O Lord. Help me to accept my entire past gracefully. Let me not blame anyone, neither myself nor anyone else. Please help me accept the past gracefully.

There are a number of things I can do, of which one I am doing right now. I can pray. I can change my attitudes.

I can change some of my personal habits, habits in thinking and in behaviour which cause recurring problems.

Let me have the will and effort necessary to fulfil it so that I can bring about the desirable changes in my life. Let me be objective enough to drop any false ideas and concepts held by me against all evidence because of my emotional attachment to them. Let me have the courage and the honesty to drop ideas, beliefs and speculations.

May I be open enough to explore, to know where there is a valid belief. May I understand it as a valid belief. May I not be confused between a fact and a belief, nor between a valid and a baseless belief.

May I have the ability to change, to reshuffle. Let me not be afraid to be wrong. Let me not be afraid to face the fact that my forefathers and my parents might have been wrong. May I have the love to know, the love to be objective.

> *O Lord*
> *Give me the will*
> *Courage*
> *Honesty*
> *And sincerity of purpose*
> *To change what I can change.*

8

A prayer is always from an individual. It is never from the self, *ātmā* but from the individual, *jīva*, who is in act the *ātmā*. It is this individual who prays.

To whom does the individual pray? I do not pray to another individual. Other individuals also have the limitations that I have as an individual. The power and knowledge of the one I pray to are free from any limitation.

Let there be no confusion about whom the individual is praying to. The self? The individual is the self. The self is not an individual, but the individual is the self.

Therefore the prayer is not towards the self but towards the self as Īśvara. The self that is now an individual is praying to the self that is Īśvara, the total, the Lord.

Let there be no confusion. A prayer is always to the Lord. Even the enlightened person who knows the meaning of the sentence, '*tat tvam asi*, you are that,' can offer a prayer as an individual because the difference between Īśvara, the Lord, and *jīva*, the individual, is evident, even though, in actual fact, there is no difference.

Non-difference between the Lord and the individual is a matter for knowledge. That the difference is apparent, *mithyā*, must be recognised. But, now, as an individual, when I see myself helpless, I cannot but pray. So, prayer is not against the teaching. In fact, any form of ritual is also a kind of prayer and is not against the teaching. I pray because I seek help. Therefore, the prayer is never to the laws themselves but to the laws as the Lord. Therefore, the prayer is always to the Lord, the maker of the world and its laws. Even a prayer directed to a deity, with reference to a given phenomenon, like sun, water, fire, and so on, goes to the Lord.

O Lord
I seek help
In order to accept my past
The past is not a villain
Nor does it have to be looked upon
With contempt
The past makes me what I am

Every experience
Was an enriching experience
The problem is
Not that I have a past
But that I see myself

As a victim of the past

Because I do not accept it

   Let it be clear

I do not hate my past.

In hatred, there is denial of the past, rejection of the past. I cannot deny my past, much less reject it. The past has happened. It is an already established fact. I cannot do anything to alter the fact. The problem is that when I reject the past, when I resent anything about the past, I do not accept the past.

When I criticise myself, I criticise the past. It means I do not accept the past. The more I am able to see how the past cannot change, the more I become free of my resentments, anger, remorse, and so on.

We spend our time and energy resenting the past. I seek help here because it is one thing to understand the past but quite another to be free from resentment and anger towards it. Prayer does something because there is submission.

Prayer itself is an action, and its result is called grace. I create the grace. I do not wait for grace to come. I invoke it by prayer. That I pray also produces a result because there is acknowledgment of my own helplessness in the submission.

If I understand how I cannot change my past, why am I angry? Why do I hate myself? Why do I criticise myself? Well, I am helpless. In the acknowledgment of helplessness and in the capacity to pray is my effort, my will. My will is used prudently in submitting. In submission, it is the will that is submitted, and to submit my will, I use my will.

One has to see the beauty of prayer. There is no meditation, no ritual, without prayer. There is no technique which can replace prayer because in any technique the will is retained. Here, the will willingly submits and submission performs the miracle. In the submission there is an acceptance. Understand that in the submission there is acceptance of the past.

I do not change the self -criticising mind. I do not want a mind that will not criticise me or anyone else. It is not the issue for me. All I want is to accept that mind. Let me accept the self-criticising mind.

When I say I accept my past, then I accept the outcome of the past. The outcome is self-criticism. I accept the mind as it is. I am not afraid of the self-judging mind, self-condemning mind. I seek total acceptance of the self-criticising mind.

O Lord
Help me accept
The mind
The self-judging
Self-criticising
Self-condemning
Self-pitying mind

Please help me
I submit my will
Because I have tried
To use my will
To change

It did not work
It will never work

I give up
I give up not helplessly
I give up prudently
And deliver myself

My will
Into your hands

I have no reason for despair
All I seek is acceptance
Of the past
With its outcome

I am not avoiding self-criticism
I do not seek your grace
To stop self-criticism
I seek your grace
To accept self-criticism.

9

Acceptance of the past implies accepting the outcome of the past. If there is an innate anger or sadness, it is the outcome of the past. Sometimes anger and sadness are manifest; sometimes they are not. When I want to accept the past, I also accept the outcome. My manifest anger, pain, depression and so on, stem from the past. My prayer to the Lord is to help me accept the past along with its outcome.

I am not interested in changing a given habit of thinking. I am interested in accepting the habit. Acceptance may bring about a change in the habit. If a change happens, it happens, but it is not why I pray.

> *O Lord*
> *I pray for serenity*
> *To gracefully accept*
> *My entire past and its outcome.*

What I have to change is my attitude. The prayer to accept the past with its outcome is for a change of attitude on my part towards my past, towards my mind, towards people, money, the future, and towards my health and body. If these attitudes cause problems, let me change.

Let me have the will and the courage to change my beliefs if they require change, blind beliefs, beliefs which are not valid because of the evidence against them. We tend to hold on to such beliefs because we have invested our time and heart in nursing them. Let me have the honesty and the courage to drop these nursed, false beliefs. Let me change these beliefs for those that are valid. Let me see the difference between valid and false beliefs. Let my commitment to the pursuit of knowledge be unflinching.

I am not interested in changing the condition of my mind. I am interested in changing my understanding, my attitudes. To know what I can change and what I cannot change is as important as acceptance and change. Without the knowledge of what I cannot change, I cannot accept. What will I accept? Nor, without knowledge, can I strive to change what I can.

When I blame someone for what was done to me in the past, it means that I want the past to be different. It cannot be different. It cannot become different. Pain and anger were my responses to situations in the past that make me blame. In blaming, I retain my pain and anger. If I refuse to blame, not with my will but with understanding, with my heart, then there is acceptance.

Let me see clearly that I cannot change the situations that have caused me pain. I cannot change the fact that I was subject to pain. I continue to retain the pain by blaming, I can drop it. I see clearly the wisdom in accepting the past. I see clearly how I can bring about changes in my understanding of the realities with reference to world, God, and me. I strive for that understanding. May my time and energy be directed towards changing what I can, and not towards changing what I cannot.

> *O Lord*
> *I stay with the present*
> *I am aware*
> *Of what happens now.*

10

We use a number of techniques for changing the condition of the mind. Prayer, however, is not a technique. Prayer is centred on the person, the total person, and it comes from the person who sees very clearly his or her helplessness in a given situation.

I may use techniques but I realise my helplessness because the situation is not centred on my will or even on my understanding. I realise the helplessness of the situation. I give up not to despair but into the hands of the Lord. The whole person that is me submits to the Lord. This is the meaning of surrender, the meaning of the situation, '*namaste astu bhagavan*, O Lord, may this salutation be unto you.'

I see an order. I did not create the order, which is the world. I am born into the order. I am a part of this order. The order has been; the order is. In this order I find myself an integral part. Because neithr I, nor any like me authored this order, I appreciate its authorship in a being that is all-knowledge; in a being we call God, the Lord. The Lord cannot be out there, outside the world, because there is no place outside the world. Nor can the Lord be in a corner of the world, like me.

If the Lord is the author of the world, the world is not separate from the Lord. The Lord is the maker as well as the material of this world. The Lord being the material cause, the world cannot be separate from the Lord. The order is of the Lord; the order is the Lord. To that order I submit. To the Lord I submit. The Lord's form includes my physical body, mind and senses. His knowledge includes my knowledge. The power he wields includes my power. The Lord is all. My submission is merely acceptance of the Lord being all.

As an individual, when I see myself helpless, I seek help from the Lord to gracefully accept what I cannot change. I do not want to change my mind. All that I care about is the capacity to accept gracefully what I cannot change.

I realise there are a number of things I cannot change, but still I wish they were different. I wish I were born in a different era. I wish I were a male. I wish I were a female. I wish I were born an only child. I wish I had a few brothers and sisters. I wish I had been understood as a child. I wish I had had a home where there was a better order and more understanding. I wish my parents had better means. I wish I had a better education. I wish I had studied when I was supposed to study. I wish I had chosen another profession. I wish this marriage had taken place. I wish my physical body were a couple of inches taller. I wish I had blond hair. I wish I were born in a different society. I wish I had a religion I could own. I wish the concept of God was not of one who punishes. I wish I could pray.

Even such a wishing mind is one that resists acceptance. Any overt expressed wish, or a lurking, vague wish, any wish at all, with reference to the past, is a will to change what I cannot change. Even the Lord cannot change what has already happened. I can lose my memory of the past, but all the riches of the experiences would be lost in the process. In fact, I submit myself to the Lord, praying for his help to accept gracefully what I cannot change.

> *O Lord*
> *Help me totally*
> *Accept my entire past*
>
> *If I have had rounds of births*
> *Help me accept all of them.*

11

There are different types of acceptance. When I accept the past, what type of acceptance is it? Is it an acceptance with reluctance? Is it an acceptance with resentment or is it just a plain, simple acceptance? When I accept with resentment or reluctance, my attitude toward what is accepted is distinct. When I accept totally, the frame of mind is different. A job given to me that I do not like, I accept with either reluctance or resentment. But when someone offers me a flower, I accept it totally with thankfulness and cheerfulness.

The frame of mind necessary for acceptance is one that obtains when I accept something cheerfully, as I do when I accept certain aspects of nature like the mountains, trees or sky. To understand such a frame of mind, imagine a clear blue sky or a night sky lit up by the moon, stars and planets, all of them shining, glittering. I do not want the sky to be different, much less the stars, the moon, and those floating clouds and cloudlets. Nor do I want myself to be different. There is total acceptance.

Here, I am totally objective; my wants, my likes and dislikes are resolved. I do not blame the sky. I do not blame anything.

I am totally objective. I accept what is. If I have to accept my past, all these characters, people and situations that comprise my past, played roles in making my past, I accept them as I accept the sky. Can I, with the same frame of mind, accept the people who played roles in my past? Each one has contributed to my past, to my hurt, to my pain and to my sorrow.

While I acknowledge their contribution, I cannot afford to blame any of them. Each one acted as he or she did because of his or her past. No one could do more than what he or she did. As a child, I could not do better either. Therefore, I accept the child in me and my interpretation of the various situations. I totally accept each of the people involved. I come to bear upon any given person with the same frame of mind that obtains when I see a clear blue sky.

I accept my mother, her problems, her attitudes and her lack of sensitivity with the same frame of mind. I accept my father, his problems, his habits, his anger, his lack of thoughtfulness. I have no difficulty in accepting their virtues. The problem is only with reference to the person's lack of thoughtfulness and sensitivity.

Each person is as he or she can be. No one can be more than what one is. I accept the fire as it is, hot. I accept it and deal with it. So too, objectively, I accept my father and mother, my sisters and brothers.

All these people who have come into my life, contributing some degree of pain in one way or the other, all of them I accept. I do it knowing full well that each one has caused me a degree of pain. I do not say they were angels. I do not say they were good to me. I acknowledge their roles in causing me pain. At the same time, I accept them objectively as they are, as they were, my teachers, co-students, friends, boyfriends and girlfriends, all of whom contributed their bit to my hurt. I come to bear upon them, one by one, with the same frame of mind that obtains when I look at the sky.

I may not have the mind that obtains when a flower is offered to me. I may have such a mind later, but for now, all I want is a mind that obtains when I look at the sky, the mountains, the trees, the birds and animals in their own habitat. Just as I look at them objectively, so too, I accept each individual as I recall each of them. It is a thorough process. I do not leave out anyone. I do not blame anyone.

Generally, we blame ourselves. It is another mistake. I do not blame myself. I was totally helpless in my childhood and often helpless in my later years. The personality that was formed in my childhood when I was helpless continued to interpret situations, keeping me helpless. So I am not to blame, nor do I want to blame others. I cannot afford to blame others.

O Lord
I pray to be given
A frame of mind
That will totally accept
Every individual
I have been connected to
And affected by

Each one
Is only as he or she can be
I blame none of them

O Lord
Give me the frame of mind
To accept these people
As they were
As they are

I do not want to change my past
Because I cannot change it

I cannot change events
That have already happened
I cannot change
My responses either

O Lord
All I seek
Is an objective frame of mind
If not a cheerful frame of mind

Please give me
An objective frame of mind
So that I can accept
All of these characters
Who played roles
In the drama of my life
What a drama!

I do not want to change the drama
It has already been staged

O Lord
Let me have the frame of mind
Which helps me look back
On the whole drama
And each of the characters

Objectively
With amusement

I do not want to change
Any of the events
Because I cannot change any of them

> *When I blame...*
> *I want to change*
> *When I complain...*
> *I want to change*
> *When I have resentment...*
> *I want to change*

O Lord
Let me have the frame of mind
That will to accept
All of these characters
And my responses to them.

12

When I accept something, what do I do? Is it just a sentence, 'I accept?' A mere sentence does not imply acceptance. Sometimes I accept something without saying so.

Acceptance implies a certain attitude on my part. When I accept something, I give it the freedom to be what it is. I do not want the thing to be different from what it is.

Acceptance implies granting freedom to the object of acceptance to be what it is. In giving freedom I do not demand the object be different from what it is. The mere word, acceptance, without understanding its implications does not help. I accept a child as the child is. I accept a tree. I accept the sun, the moon. I accept a bird, its colour, its behaviour. I accept a chemical as it is. I accept sugar as it is. I accept poison as it is. Acceptance does not imply that I have to use it. In acceptance, there is objectivity. I let things be as they are.

With reference to my past, however, I do not let it be as it is. I do not accept it because the past has caused me pain. Due to my helplessness I subjected myself to pain, to hurt. Therefore, the painful past is not acceptable to me. Can I bring myself to accept the past? When I bring myself to bear upon the past, can I be the same person that I am when I accept the sky?

How do I accept the sky? What frame of mind do I have when I accept the sky? The same frame of mind I bring to bear upon my mother and father, whether they are alive or not. In the same way, I accept my friends, my relatives, employers, my grand parents, my children and my partner in life. Individually, I accept every one of them because I give them the freedom to be what they are. I do not blame the sky because it is or is not blue.

I bring the same person to bear upon those with whom my life has been cast. They are all different characters in the drama of my life. I free myself from blaming any one of them. I blame no one, nor do I blame myself.

O Lord
Please give me
The serenity
The clarity
To accept gracefully
What I cannot change
And change what I can

I cannot change the past
For it has already happened

But I can change my attitudes
My understanding

I can bring about a change
In my attitude
Towards the world
By widening
My understanding

Let me change
What I can

O Lord
Grant me the wisdom
To know the difference
Between what I can
And cannot change

In so many words, I pray.

Oṁ tat sat

Books by Swami Dayananda Saraswati

Public Talk Series :
1. Living Intelligently
2. Need for Cognitive Change
3. Discovering Love
4. Successful Living
5. The Value of Values
6. Vedic View and Way of Life

Upaniṣad Series :
7. Muṇḍakopaniṣad Vol 1 & 2
8. Kenopaniṣad

Moments with Oneself Series :
9. Freedom from Helplessness
10. Living versus Getting On
11. Insights
12. Action and Reaction
13. The Fundamental Problem
14. Problem is You, Solution is You
15. Purpose of Prayer
16. Vedanta 24x7
17. Freedom
18. Crisis Management
19. Surrender and Freedom
20. The Need for Personal Reorganisation
21. Freedom in Relationship
22. Stress-free Living

Text Translation Series :

23. Śrīmad Bhagavad Gītā

   (Text with roman transliteration and English translation)

Stotra Series :

24. Dipārādhanā

25. Prayer Guide

   (With explanations of several Mantras, Stotras, Kirtans and Religious Festivals)

Bhagavad Gītā Series :

26. Bhagavad Gītā Home Study Program
   Vol 1-4 (Hardbound)

27. Bhagavad Gītā Home Study Program
   Vol 1-4 (Softbound)

Meditation Series :

28. Morning Meditation-prayers

Essays :

29. Do all Religions have the same goal?

30. Conversion is Violence

31. Gurupūrṇimā

32. Dānam

33. Japa

34. Can We?

35. **Teaching Tradition of Advaita Vedanta**

Exploring Vedanta Series : (*vākyavicāra*)

36. śraddhā bhakti dhyāna yogād avaihi
    ātmānaṁ ced vijānīyāt

BOOKS BY SMT. SHEELA BALAJI

37. Salutations to Rudra
    (based on the exposition of Śrī Rudram by
    Swami Dayananda Saraswati)

38. Without a Second

Also available at :

ARSHA VIDYA RESEARCH
AND PUBLICATION TRUST
32/4 Sir Desika Road
Mylapore Chennai 600 004
Telefax : 044 - 2499 7131
Email : avrandpc@gmail.com
ARSHA VIDYA GURUKULAM
P.O.Box 1059. Pennsylvania
PA 18353, USA.
Ph : 001-570-992-2339
Email : avp@epix.net

ARSHA VIDYA GURUKULAM
Anaikatti P.O.
Coimbatore 641 108
Ph : 0422 - 2657001
Fax : 0422 - 2657002
Email : office@arshavidya.in
SWAMI DAYANANDA ASHRAM
Purani Jhadi, P.B. No. 30
Rishikesh, Uttaranchal 249 201
Telefax : 0135-2430769
Email : ashrambookstore@yahoo.com

AND IN ALL THE LEADING BOOK STORES, INDIA